T0370204

NEW EXPANDED EDITION

Conquering the Beast Within

How I Fought Depression and Won... And How You Can, Too

One teenager tells her inspiring story

CAIT IRWIN

Conquering the Beast Within

How I Fought Depression and Won...And How You Can, Too

Cait Irwin

ISBN: 979-8-35097-053-1

© 2024. All rights reserved. No part of this publication may be reproduced, distributed, or transmitted in any form or by any means, including photocopying, recording, or other electronic or mechanical methods, without the prior written permission of the publisher, except in the case of brief quotations embodied in critical reviews and certain other noncommercial uses permitted by copyright law.

For Mom.

Thank you for always believing in me, I love you.

If you are reading this, please know that you have already demonstrated a profound amount of courage. It tells me that you WANT to get better, and/or that you want to understand what a loved one is going through. In all my years working through my own issues, as well as trying to do my part to destigmatize mental illness in general, I have seen so many people do everything they can to avoid facing their beast. They would never imagine picking up a book like this, thinking that it will just go away because it is too scary to face...but it will not simply go away, and you have the wisdom to know that. So here you are looking at the beast right in the eye! Again, I am truly inspired by your courage.

This is my own personal story, and your story will be as unique as YOU. The lessons you learn will also be unique but no matter what, the feeling of empowerment you gain from your own healing process will show you a strength that you never thought you had. You will use that strength for the rest of your life and that will most certainly inspire others!

We all have arrived at this point for different reasons, but we are united in an understanding of how this "beast" can wreak havoc in our hearts and minds. I wrote and illustrated this book over 30 years ago (at age 14), but the feeling and impact of depression is timeless. When trying to decide if I should republish my original book, I circled back to my original intention of creating this book, what began as my personal journal(sketchbook) as a way to use my authentic voice and drawings to communicate with the ones closest to me about what was going on inside of me... as well as embracing my own personal fears to share my story with the world. My hope is that helps others feel that they are not alone in their pain and that it is possible to recover, understand, manage and even learn from your beast.

In order to preserve my perspective as a teenager, the original text and illustrations have been kept the same. However, I thought it would be useful to expand the original book with a few new thoughts and illustrations because I am a person who has dealt with their beast most of their adult life. A lot can happen in 30 years, but many things have remained the same for me... I still use art to express myself with humor, creativity, and vulnerability. Republishing this book has served to deepen my well of empathy and I hope that you can FEEL that through my work.

-Cait

"You have seen my descent.
Now watch my rising"
Rumi

TABLE OF CONTENTS

CHAPTER ONE

A BEAST IS BORN

In our minds stalks a beast...a cruel, mean and wicked beast. This beast loves to hate. He is that feeling you have when you say, "I give up", or "I hate myself" or "I don't want to live." He loves to devour your good feelings.

He eats everything that matters to you til you are left with nothing.

The beast is depression.

During my personal struggle with depression I began to see a wild and ferocious beast as a symbol of my illness. Seeing the beast as a separate being helped me to understand and cope with the way I was feeling. Hopefully, my perspective of the beast will help you and those around you understand the illness, its emotions, reactions, and feelings, which may be hard to explain.

I had to make a decision to either challenge the beast or give in to him. Sometimes you might think that it's easier just to give up and live with depression, or give up and let go of life. I decided to challenge him every day until I won. You have the courage and persistence in your heart to challenge your beast and be a winner.

Some people refer to depression as a mental illness or brain disorder. I call it my broken leg theory. Let me explain. While I was depressed I missed a lot of things; the many great times I could have had with my friends and family; a bunch of school; and my favorite sports. I basically felt like I had missed a huge portion of my life. I felt terrible but my friends and family helped me to realize that what I have is an illness, just like having a broken leg. If you broke your leg you would miss out on some school and sports and other activities. You'd still have to do a lot of work to get better. If you had a serious disease like cancer you would have to do a lot of work to feel better, like taking medicine and enduring pain, (physical and mental). Just remember your depression, the beast, is just as serious and real.

The most important thing to remember about depression and the beast is that...You and the beast are not the same, you are two separate beings. It's perfectly clear it's not your fault nor is it a character flaw.

You are you!

And the beast is depression.

The first question you ask is "why me?" You may be feeling you did something wrong... Like you're being punished. The reality is you didn't do anything wrong, but it's tough to believe it.

I asked the question "why me" many times, but you have to realize it's not a punishment and you don't deserve it. It's an illness just like the flu and you don't have control over getting it. But society tends to look at mental illness differently from a physical illness.

NOTE:

Depression is not a weakness, it's an illness that's treatable.

The "beauty" of depression is there's so much more to gain than lose from the experience.

The feeling you'll get when you face and defeat the beast is worth the fight. When your battle is won you'll be able to face anything on the horizon.

What's causing it?

When I first found out I was depressed, I kept wondering when did it start? Then it hit me, I had been depressed for about a year. The reason I didn't notice it before was because in the beginning the illness starts out small. I thought nothing about it, perhaps a bad day, and I accepted it because I thought it was a part of my life. But it grew rapidly. The sadness became deep and was unstoppable for weeks at a time. It was growing inside of me and got big before I realized something was seriously wrong.

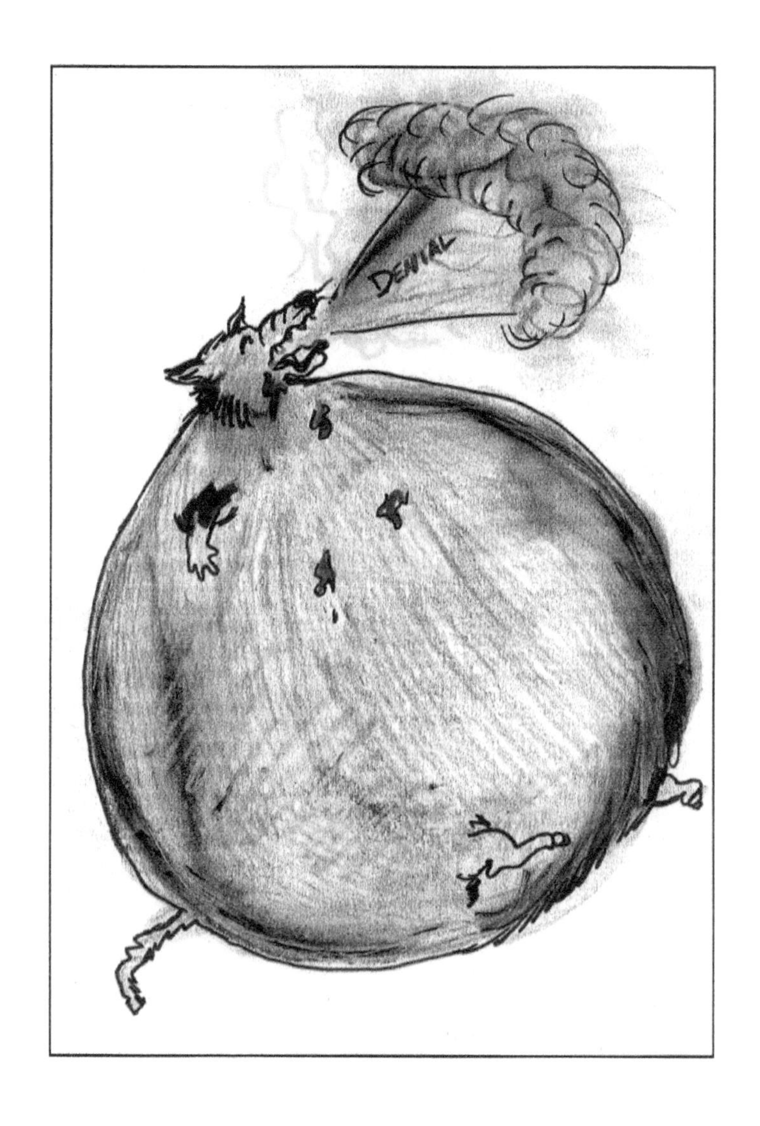

The beast had consumed me. I didn't want to admit it, so I kept it inside and kept denying that something was wrong. It was like I had invited him to an "all you can eat buffet."

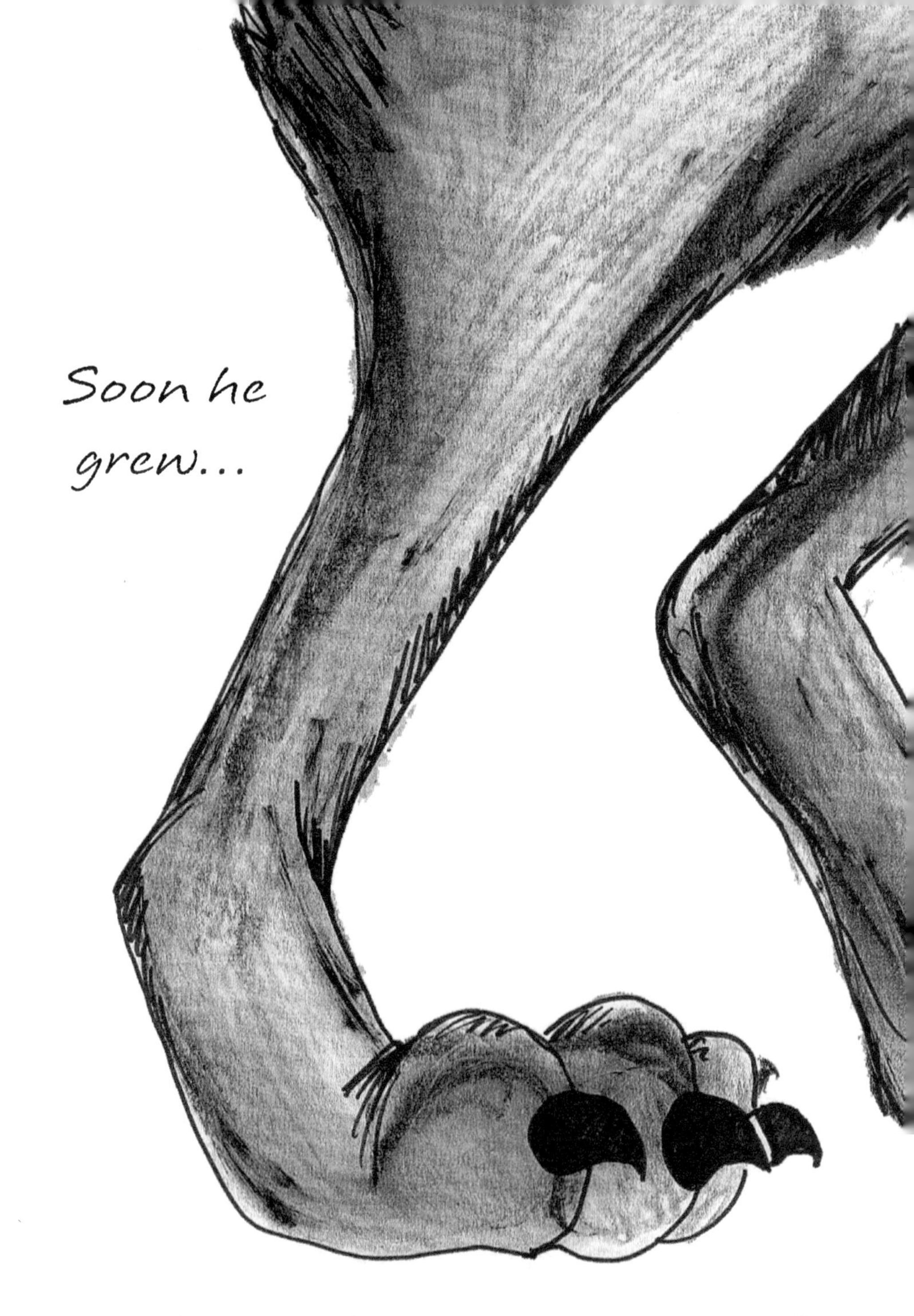

Soon he grew...

out of control...to a point where I couldn't handle it.

The beast can't stand positive feelings that are really there, like understanding, love and trust, etc. He consumes them, leaving you with negative ones like paranoia, hopelessness and especially no trust.

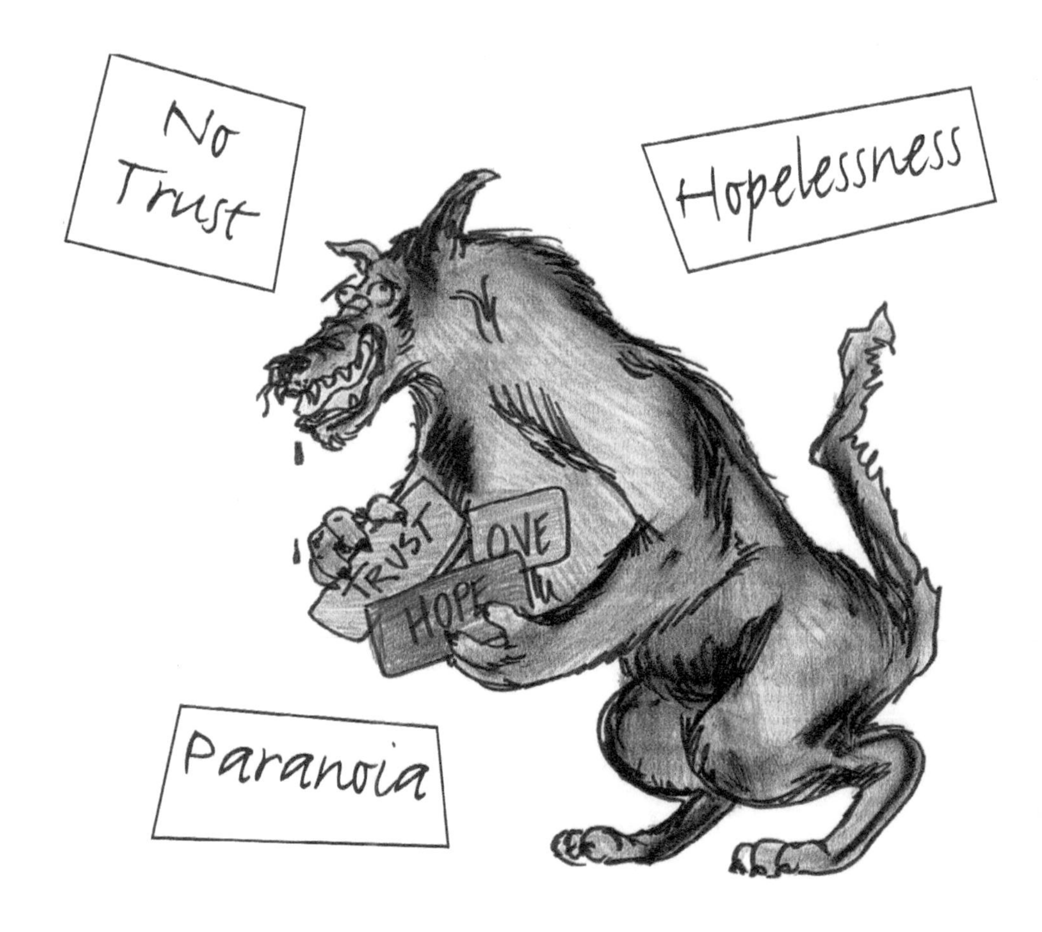

Trust is the beast's favorite meal.

Trust is so important and it's terrible when you lose it. When I lost it I couldn't even trust my family, much less my friends. I always felt they thought I was a burden and that they were talking about me. Remember that insecurity is part of the illness. Maybe a picture will help explain.

Who to trust?

He begins feasting on your self-esteem and confidence...

Then happiness...
HAPPINES

Next he feeds on your pride and dignity.

Not only does the beast eat your good feelings,

he also eats time.

There are other bad feelings that are running through your head and sometimes they're out of control. Feelings like anger...you might take it out on other people...when really you're angry at the beast.

CHAPTER

SYMPTOMS OF THE BEAST

Paranoia

Sadness...

loneliness...

you might start to feel trapped.

Frustration... Stress...

Sometimes you can't
see the real you.

Inside, you could have everything it takes to make yourself really happy, but the beast has taken everything from you, leaving you totally depressed. All you can see is... him.

The beast blinds you from many things like...

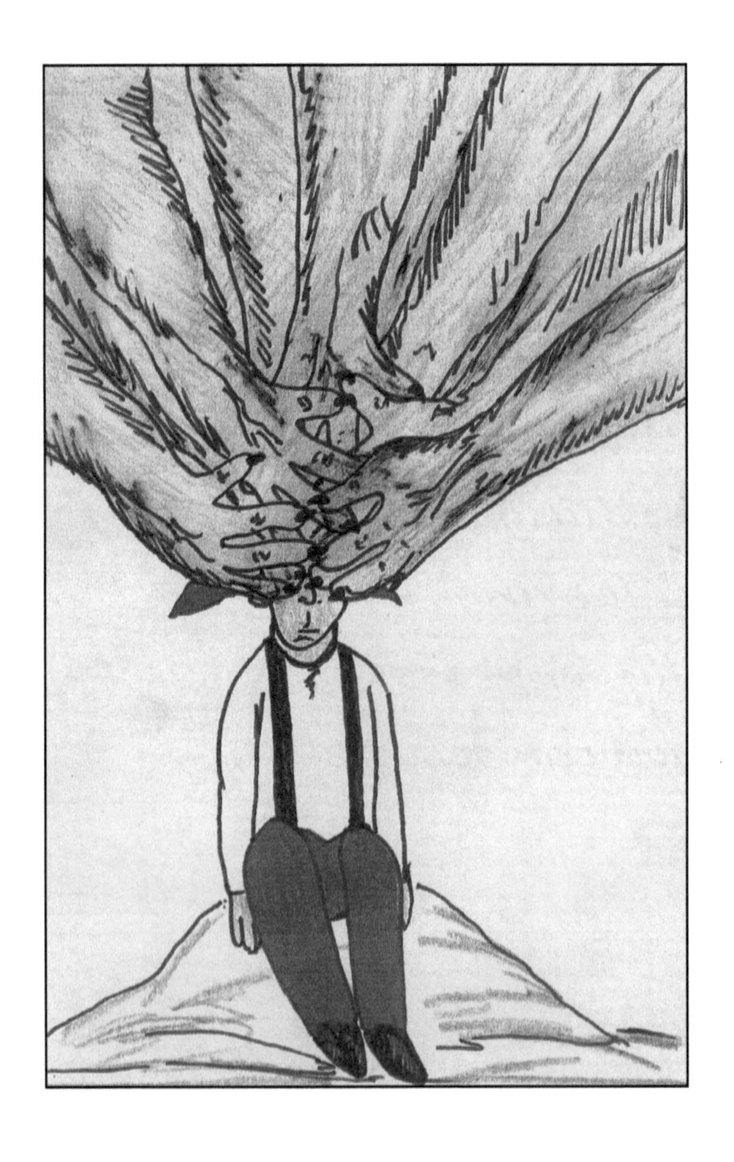

He turns the lights out on your family.

He makes your friends worry.

Family and friends are very important, but sometimes they don't understand because they may also be confused and scared.

When you're depressed it confuses everyone around you.

Sometimes depression can affect you physically, like me. I had all the symptoms, such as...

Always feeling tired and weak. You don't have any drive or ambition, nothing matters, no matter how important it is.

Some days you don't even want to leave your room.

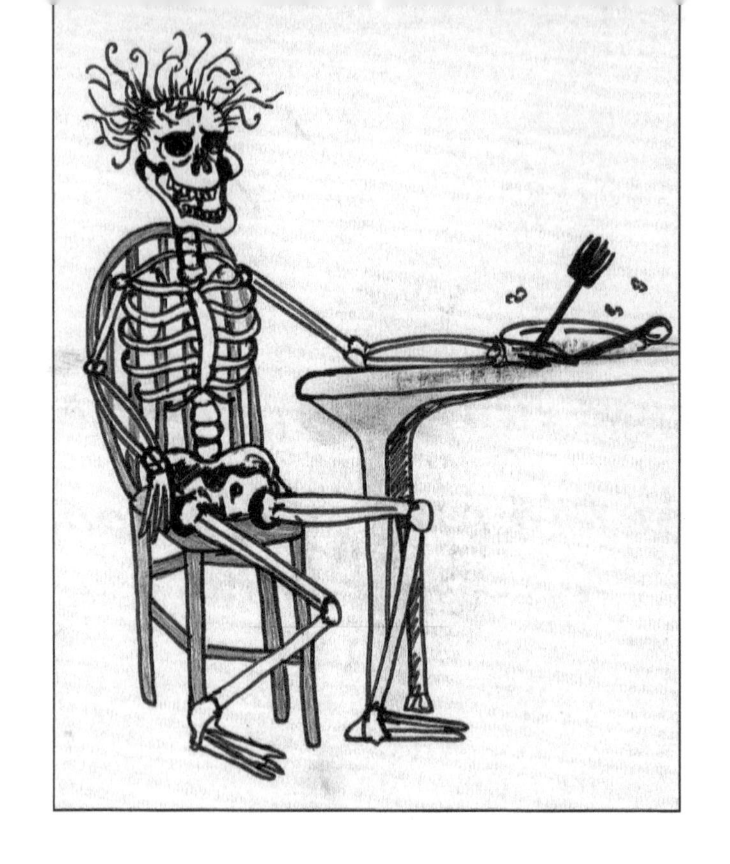

Your eating habits might change as well. I lost a lot of weight and it felt terrible. You might find yourself eating too much or not wanting to eat at all. I experienced many other symptoms too. Such as...

Slurred or slow speech

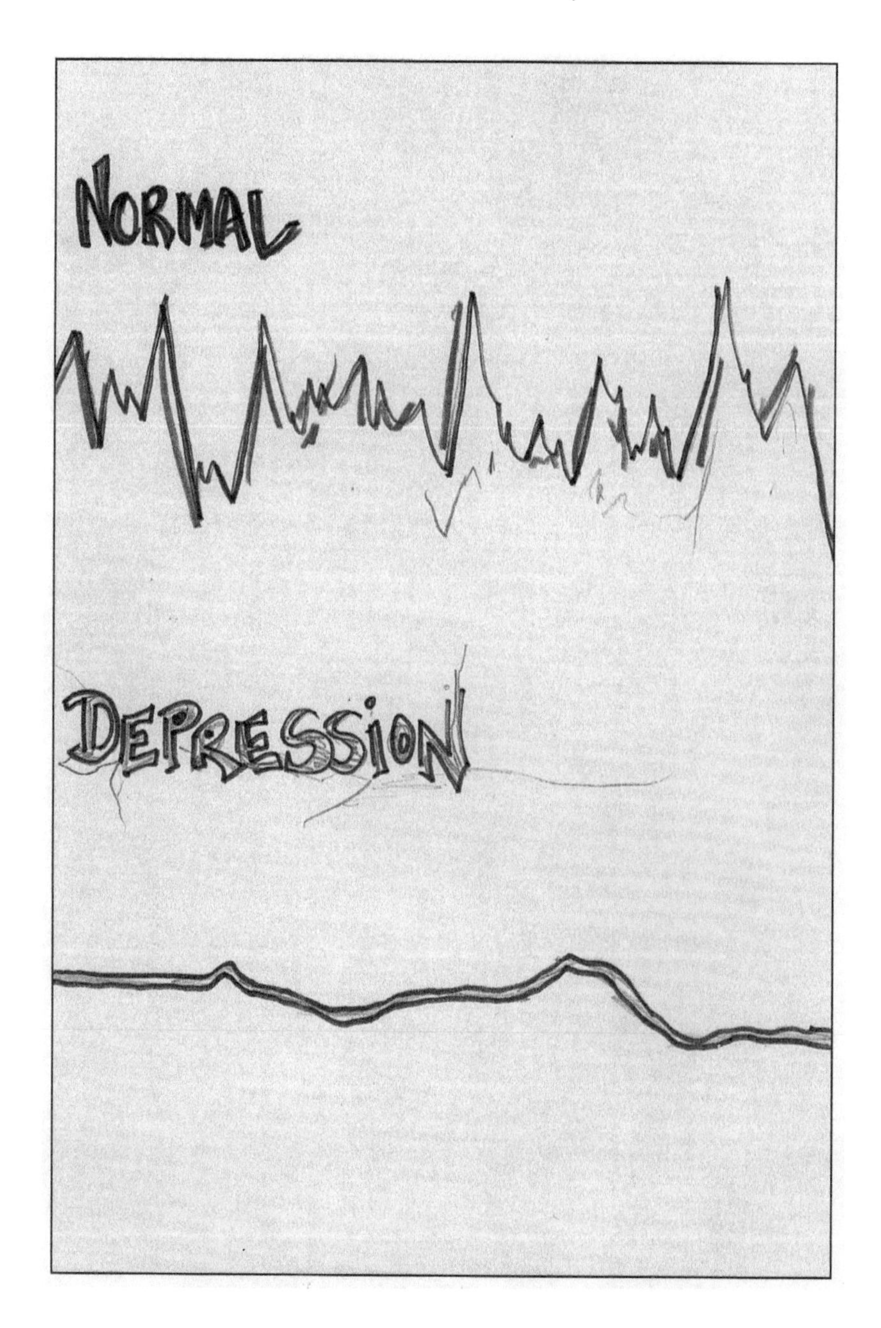

Blurred
vision

Noises seem louder than usual.

Headaches

Memory loss

Even heartburn

The beast sometimes makes it impossible to fall asleep.

And if you do finally fall asleep you have only just begun the battle...

The battle comes in the form of nightmares, one right after another...

Night after night.

Many times people lose hope.

With hope all things are possible. Without hope the beast easily wins.

That's why barbecuing hope burgers is his specialty.

CHAPTER THREE

ASK FOR HELP

Rather than ask for help, a lot of times people try to help themselves.

VODKA
Self-medications like drugs or alcohol will damage the chemistry that's already in bad shape. Many times those chemicals are what's causing your depression.

The worst (and scariest) thing is believing that suicide is the ultimate form of self-help.

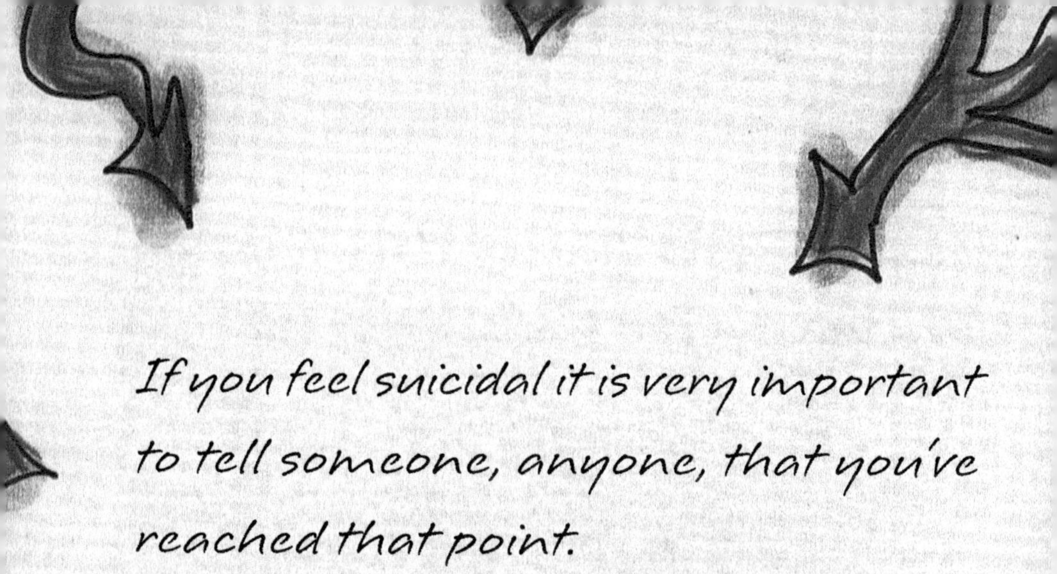

If you feel suicidal it is very important to tell someone, anyone, that you've reached that point.

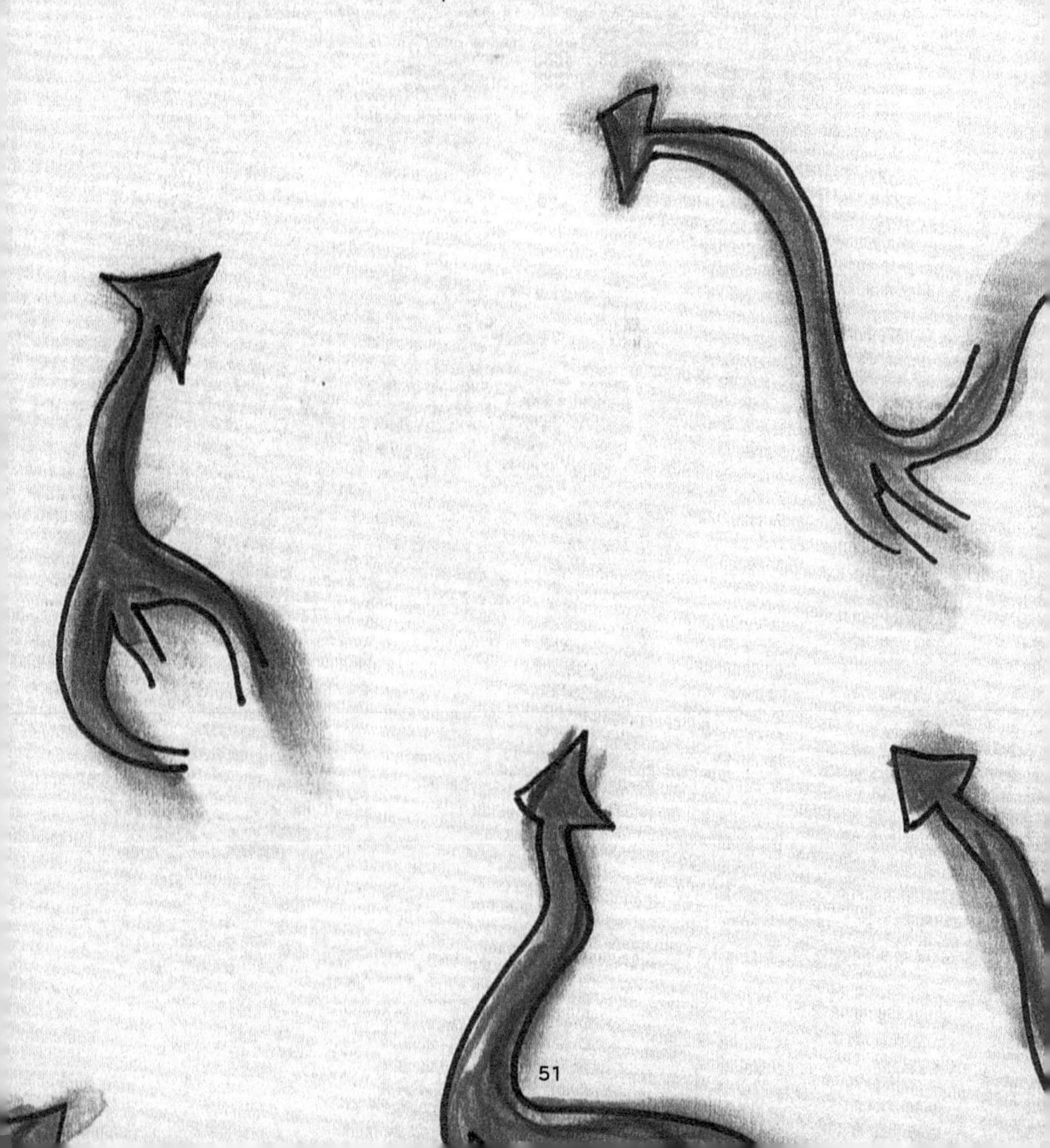

Resources for help and healing can be found in the back of this book!

CHAPTER

YOUR BATTLE BEGINS NOW!!!

As soon as you start to get help the struggle with your beast will begin. Be ready to fight hard because you are the only one who can shrink him. Here are some ways that will help you out.

Your battle
will be
extremely
scary,

but you'll find courage you thought you never had once you've made the commitment to fight. You'll find you have a Lion's heart!

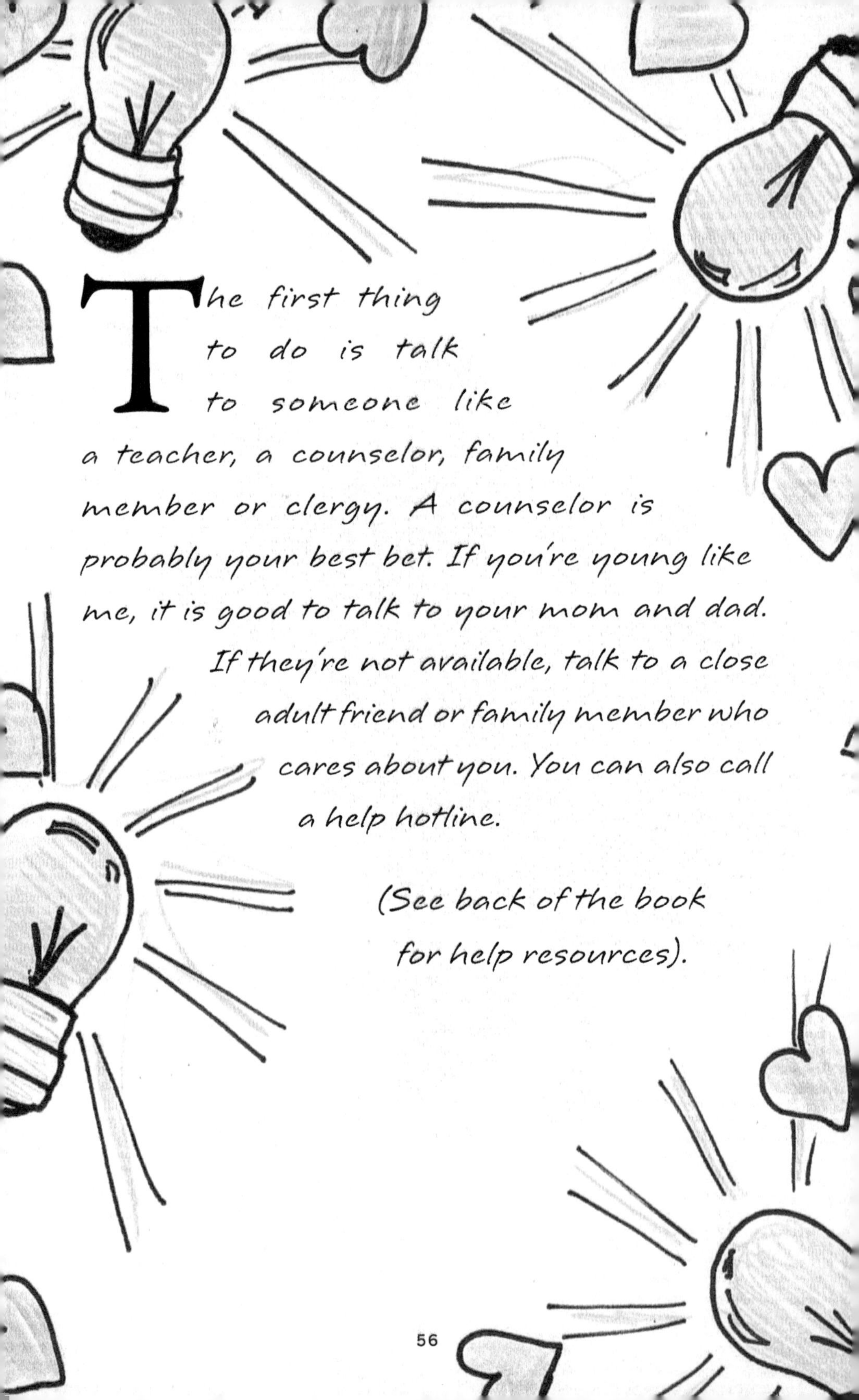

The first thing to do is talk to someone like a teacher, a counselor, family member or clergy. A counselor is probably your best bet. If you're young like me, it is good to talk to your mom and dad. If they're not available, talk to a close adult friend or family member who cares about you. You can also call a help hotline.

(See back of the book for help resources).

Counseling is a great start, but the beast hates it because he knows that it will help you. So, he plugs his ears. You may need more help, like medicine.

Medicine can help get your body chemistry back on track,

but he will do everything he can to flush your medicine down the toilet.

Sometimes when you take medicine to balance out the chemicals in your brain, it might not work. So, it might have to be changed. With me, I had to get it adjusted many times. If your prescription isn't working, don't hesitate to tell your doctor.

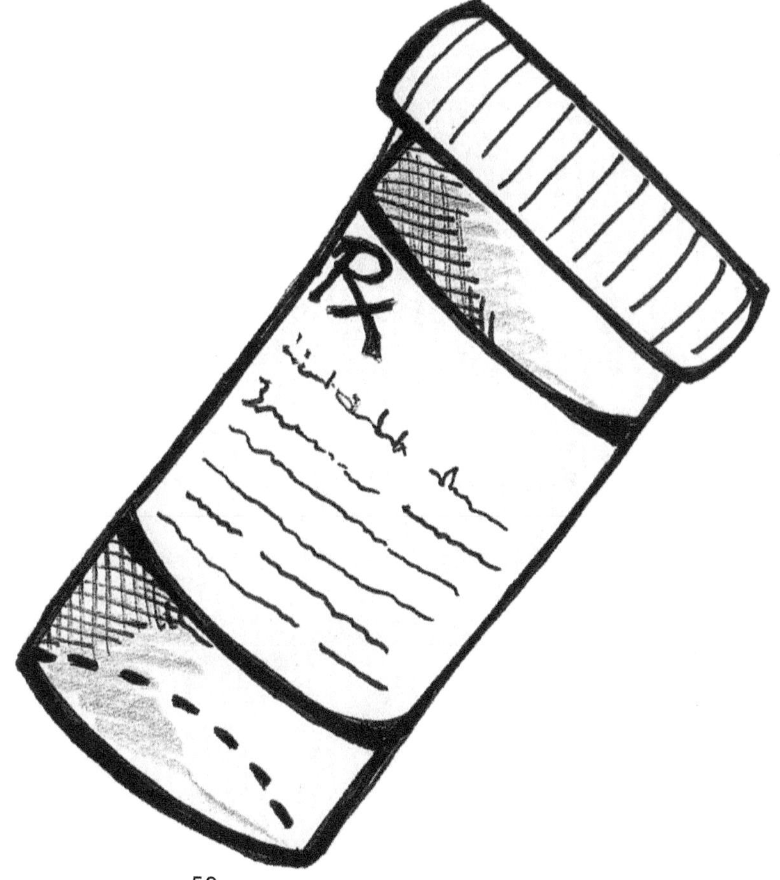

See, medicine is like poison to the beast. When he's hungry he'll go for a slab of feelings.

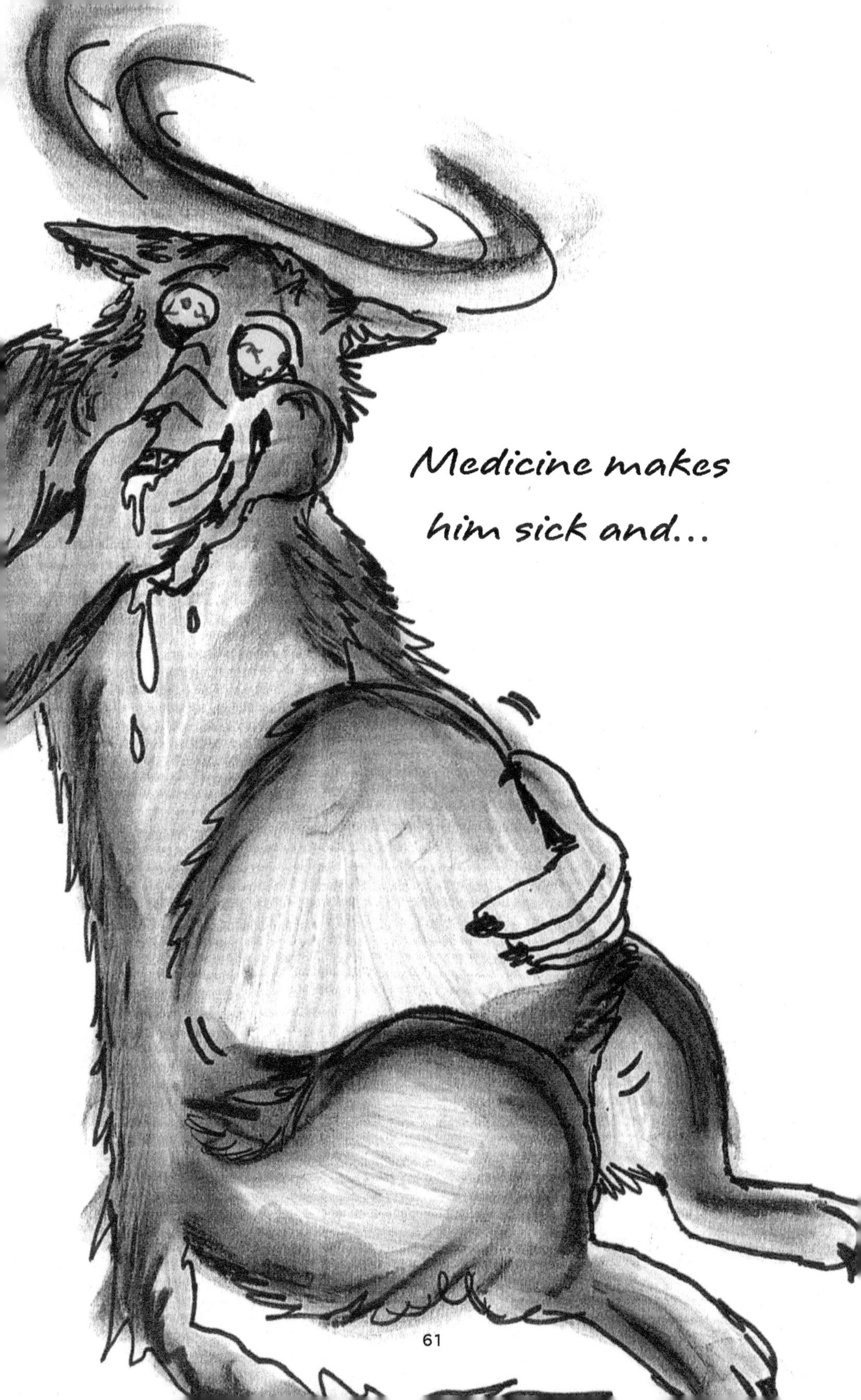
Medicine makes
him sick and...

Mad

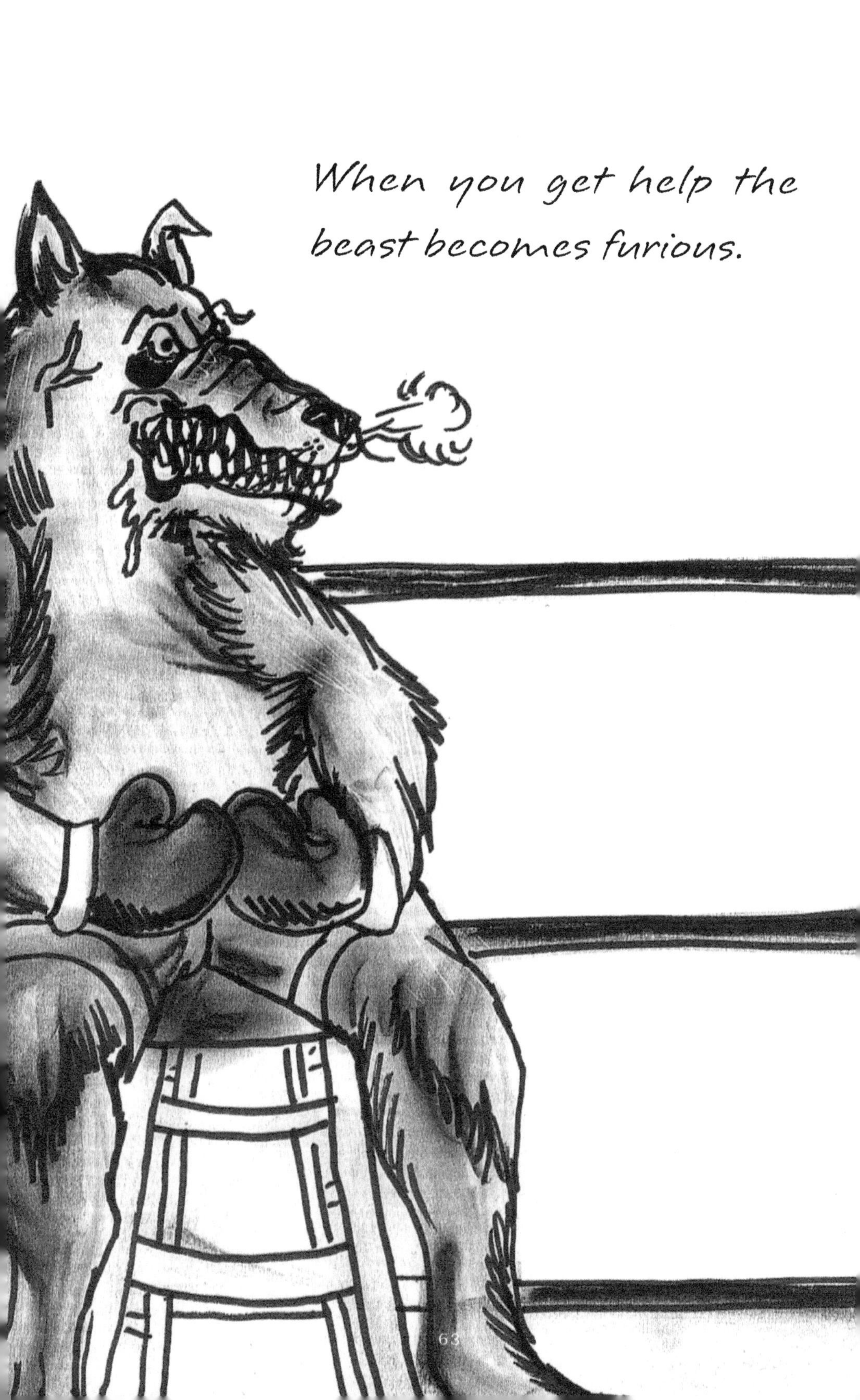
When you get help the
beast becomes furious.

He fights hard, sometimes too hard. Sometimes you might need a little more to shrink him down to size. It might take a higher dosage of medicine. If your beast is still unstoppable, you might need to go to the hospital for a little while. That's OK, just keep thinking about what will help you and what will shrink your beast.

A lot of times I felt discouraged when my medicine had to be changed so much. You will have times when you fall down on your climb to mental wellness. Don't worry. It doesn't mean you're going to be so bad off again. Be prepared. Do things you like... things that make you happy; that give you an extra burst of courage or that fill those empty spaces in you. Things like...

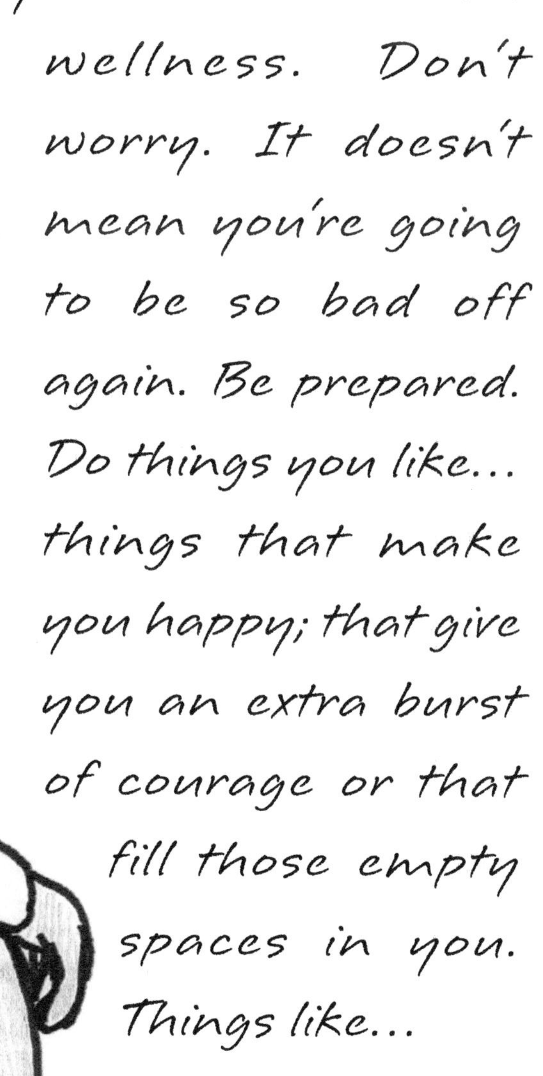

Music played a key role
in my recovery.

Listen to whatever music
helps you the most.

Watching a good TV show usually helps too. It was always calming for me to go to a movie, because it is quiet and peaceful in a theater. You can escape and get your mind off of your problems for a while.

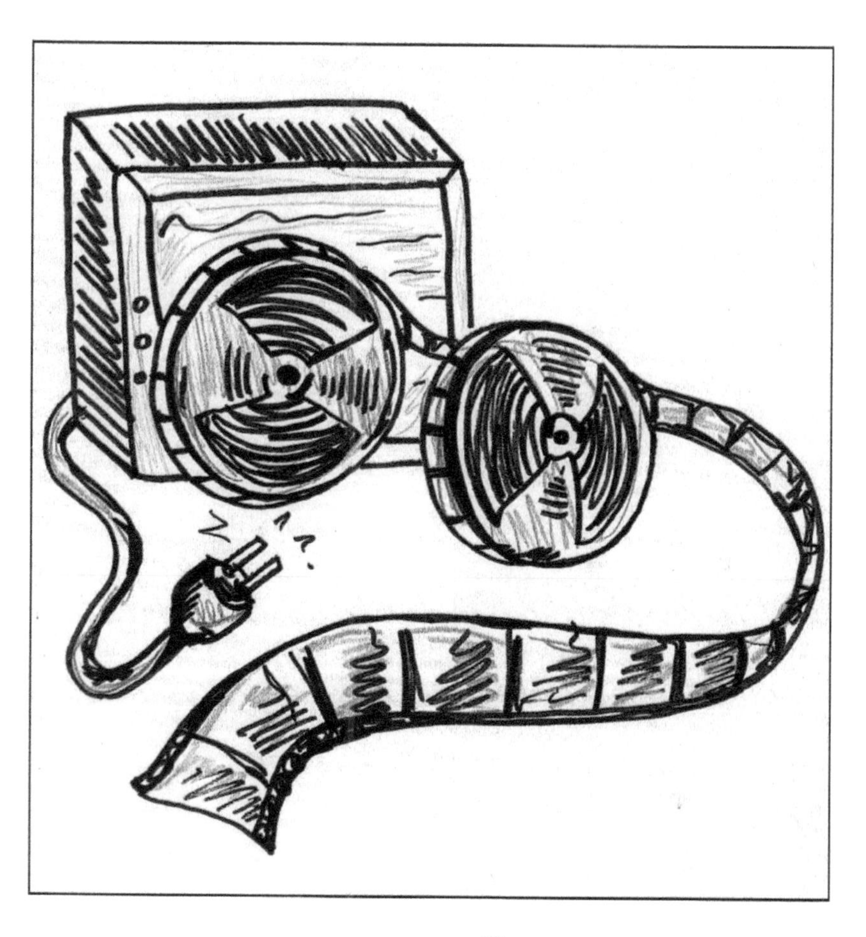

One thing that helps is to find a hobby, something that you're good at and love doing. A hobby can help you pull through. For me it was art. As a matter of fact, writing this book helped me get through my battle.

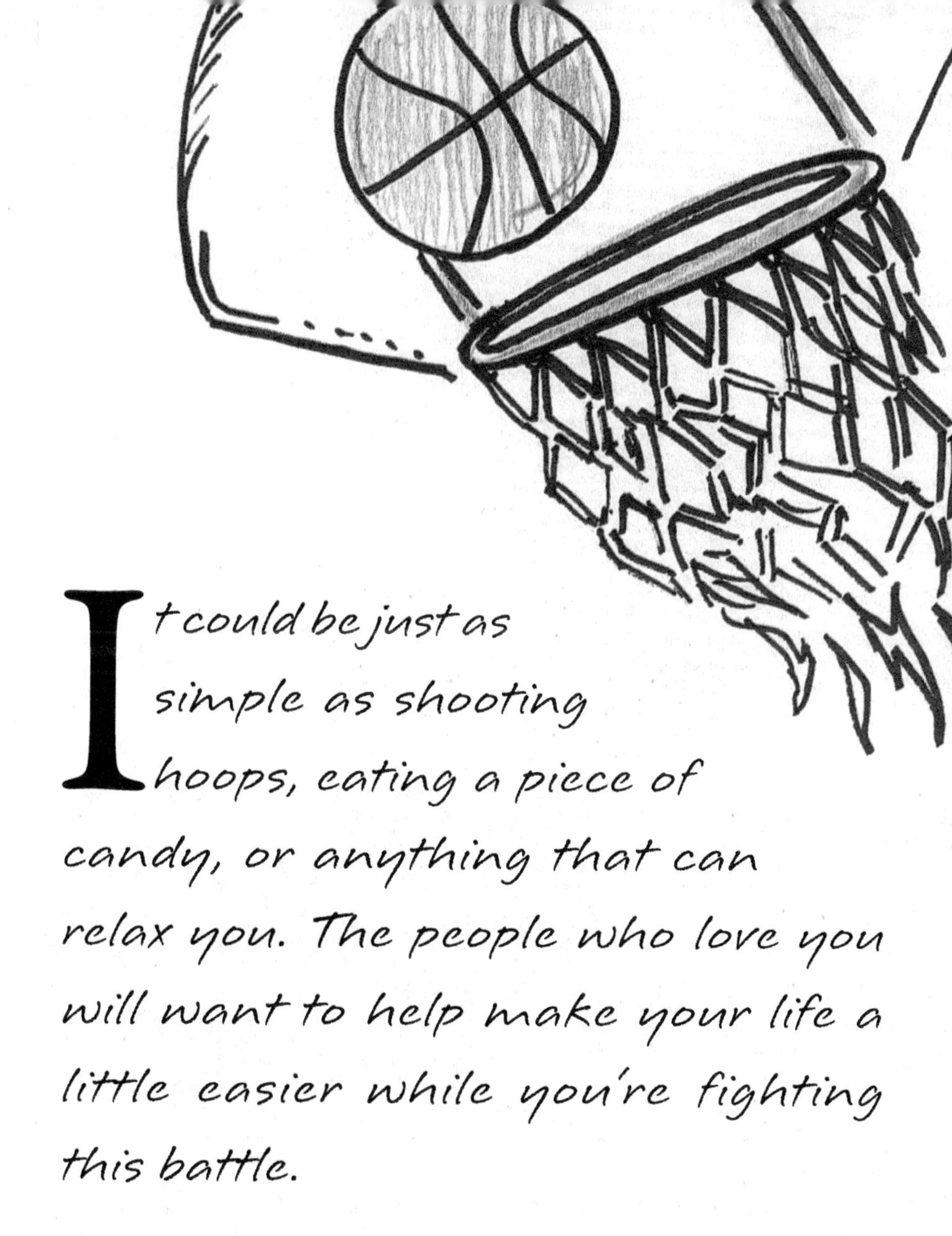

It could be just as simple as shooting hoops, eating a piece of candy, or anything that can relax you. The people who love you will want to help make your life a little easier while you're fighting this battle.

It could be going to the zoo or being out in nature.

I needed to be surrounded by animals. They helped me out a lot, especially my ferret named Glynis. Psychologists say pets can be a great help because their love is unconditional.

Some ways that you can help yourself physically are... less sugar intake. That was tough because I love sugar. It's also good to get some vitamins, especially if you have problems with eating. Check your local health food stores. Eat foods with high protein, like beans! They doooo taste so good in a bean burrito. Exercise. Yes, it's hard so start out slow and gradually build up.

CHAPTER

THERAPY, HOSPITALIZATION AND HEALING

If you have to go to the hospital, it will be scary at first, especially if you don't know what's going to happen. I'll tell you what happened to me because it may vary in some ways from hospital to hospital. The reason that I needed to check into a hospital was that I got to a point where I couldn't trust myself. I didn't know if I wanted to live or die. I went to the hospital to talk about my problems and to find the right treatment to help me. But most importantly to keep me safe.

When I arrived at the hospital it was really hard to be left there. Before my mom left, we worked out a plan for phone calls. The hospital had to approve it to make sure the people I talked to were a good influence. I was allowed two calls in the morning and two at night. I found a lot of inner courage experiencing this. My mom brought me some things from home, like my pillow and my favorite stuffed animal. The hospital staff checked everything for items which I could use to hurt myself. I got a routine check-up by the doctor who took my weight, blood pressure and all of the basics.

The first night I was in there was hard. The room didn't have anything in it except a bathroom, bed and some drawers. The next morning I had to get up bright and early. The food wasn't all that hot. The staff went over the daily schedule. Then came the hard part. A total physical. That day was probably the hardest day of all because I thought I had taken every test in the book. In the hospital I received information on the various levels of progression through their program. The more my condition improved, the more freedom I received.

Here are the levels:

- Level 1- Suicide and escape precautions
- Level 2- Still pretty strict
- Level 3- More privileges
- Level 4- Freedom

When you get to level four you're almost ready to go home. At first my family could only visit me for a couple hours during the week and on weekends. The more the staff got to know me, the more I considered them as friends, rather than superiors. I had a roommate that had already been through the system so that helped.

When I was released from the hospital, I became discouraged very easily because I felt so vulnerable. I felt a lot of pressure to be the enthusiastic person I once was...the artist, the actor, the athlete.

I had to keep on going to counseling and it's hard spilling your guts to doctor after doctor, but you've got to stick with it because medicine alone won't cure you. **You have to be Big and Brave!** The counseling will help shrink your beast.

It's ok not to agree with your therapist all the time. But, if you keep disagreeing, tell someone you trust. You may need to get a second opinion and may even need to change doctors.

We started to see a pattern within my depressive behavior. PMS symptoms and depression symptoms are almost identical. My hormone levels seemed to be making my depression twice as bad, once a month. That's the last thing you need to deal with! Talk to your therapist or psychiatrist about seeing a gynecologist. I know it's another doctor to see, but it might really help. It helped me to start taking hormone pills. They didn't interfere with my antidepressants.

CHAPTER

THE BEAST IS LEASHED

If you work hard enough, go to counseling,
take your medication and do the things that
make you happy...
N
Then you've got
him on the run!

Next, you'll be able to put him on a leash.

Pretty soon you'll be able to muzzle him so he can't eat your feelings anymore.

Hey, how about a new look?

The more you keep fighting,
the more you'll notice the beast starting to shrink!

He doesn't
like that
very much.
Too bad!

Your beast
shrinks...

Author's note:
I love seeing the beast shrink,
this can be so satisfying!

and shrinks

and shrinks a little more...

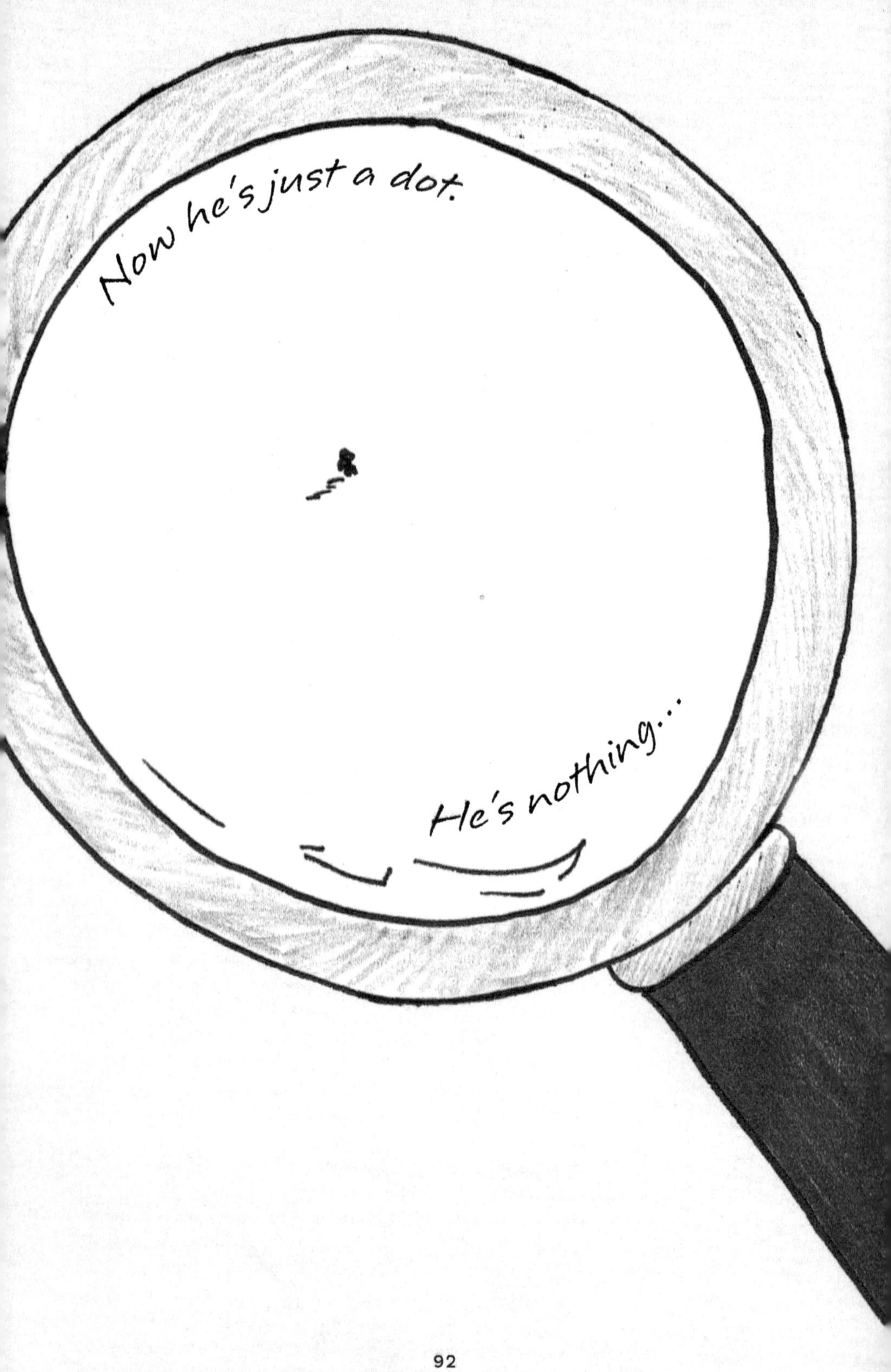
Now he's just a dot.
He's nothing...

As you begin to heal
it's like going up a
steep hill with
some
ups and
downs.

Sometimes you might have the feeling of being afraid to get better, because it seems like when you get better there's too much to face... or you won't get enough attention when you really need it. Don't worry. When you're better you will be so strong that you can face things that seemed big before and they'll be nothing. The people that care about you will always be there for you.

On your climb remember to take it slow, don't rush it.

Stop and smell the roses and pet the mountain goat.

You have gained your life back! For some strange but unbelievable reason a cat's fur feels softer, clouds make pictures of ferrets and every person, idea or thought makes your heart glow. You see things you've never noticed before...and it feels so good!

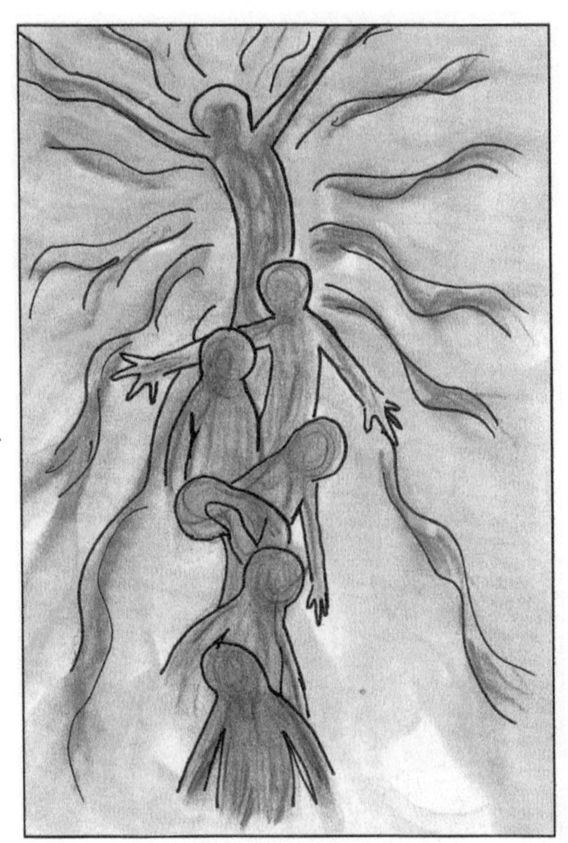

The Road Map to Victory

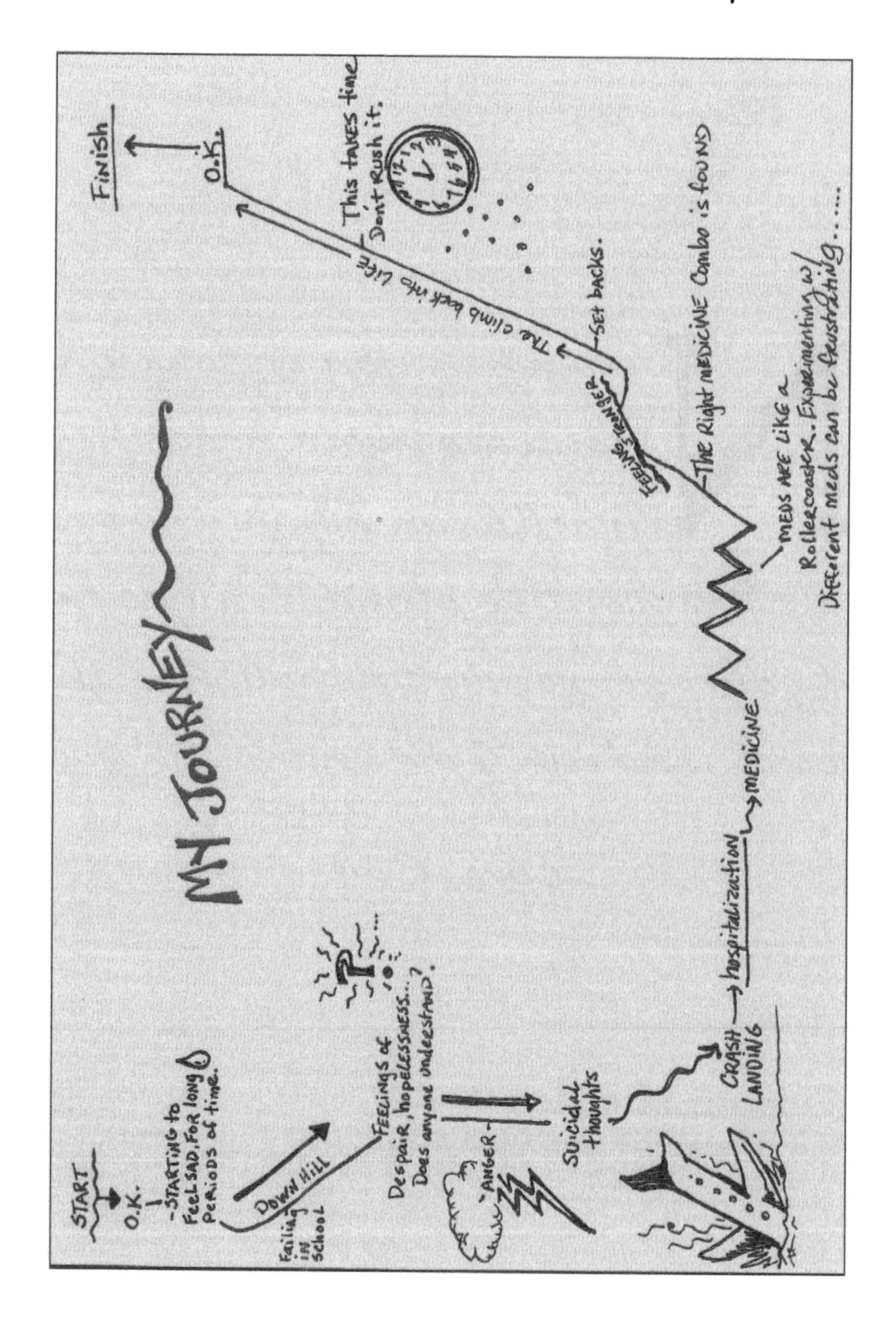

Now when you or someone you care about needs help you'll know what to do and say. You won't be afraid. You'll be full of courage, ready to challenge the beast...and win. I did and so can you.

Love, Cait

CHAPTER

THEN AND NOW

30 YEARS LATER

It would seem foolish for me to republish a book from so long ago without including some new insights on what I have learned from my many years of dealing with my beast. I am not going to lie...sometimes the beast gets big again at different points in your life, but I can assure you that you get a little wiser through experience. Especially when it comes to recognizing the presence of your beast much earlier than before.

My relationship with my beast has evolved, and at this point in my life, I feel like I have made peace with it. Although it is a part of me, it does not define me. I can now appreciate the lessons it has shown me (whether I wanted those lessons or not). It has led me to a point of deeper self-awareness, a sense of empathy, resilience, passion for living and showing up every day as the best person I can possibly be.

I do not know the answers, and I would never be so arrogant to think so, but I DO know my own story very well. So, in alignment with my intentions with the original "Conquering the Beast Within," I hope you can identify with these new illustrations, and that they make you feel seen and heard in the deepest way.

I invite you to explore your own interpretations of these illustrations first before you read mine.

THE ONLY WAY OUT IS THROUGH

This is a tough pill to swallow, but it is so true in its challenging simplicity. To some it seems too simple to believe and it can be downright trite to others. It takes a certain amount of courage to go THROUGH and deal with something head on. I have kidded myself at times that I was truly facing a problem, but I was only dancing around the edges.

However, there is a point where the idea of facing something honestly is much easier than existing with the pain of an unresolved wound. I remember reaching that point as a teenager (and many times since) where I weighed my options of which pain to carry. I also remember all the profound feelings of empowerment once I started moving THROUGH, as best as I could, without self-pity but with personal responsibility and a deep love for myself (flaws and all). Personally, I think it is easier said than done, but moving through your pain is the BEST gift you can give yourself.

THE BEAST LOOKS A BIT DIFFERENT NOW.

How the beast appears to me now has certainly changed. When I first had a vision of the beast, during the first night of my hospitalization, it was very specific and appeared as a mongrel dog of sorts. But now it is less defined as my life, relationships and responsibilities as an adult has changed my perspective. The beast appears more like an undefined vapor, vague and fluid in nature.

At times, it has been hard for me to sort out what is causing the beast to gain a bigger presence. Is it a chemical imbalance like I was diagnosed with as a teen? Or is it the stinging self-doubt when faced with new challenges? Or is it due to prolonged stress (it is a tough and often heartbreaking world to live in)? But my drive to keep living a life that brings true fulfillment, and the desire to keep moving forward despite the presence of an undefined beast, has eclipsed the all-consuming power of depression. In fact, this "dance" with the beast over the years has rekindled my commitment to honoring my soul's purpose to use my gifts for the greater good.

A HEART BREAKS FREE

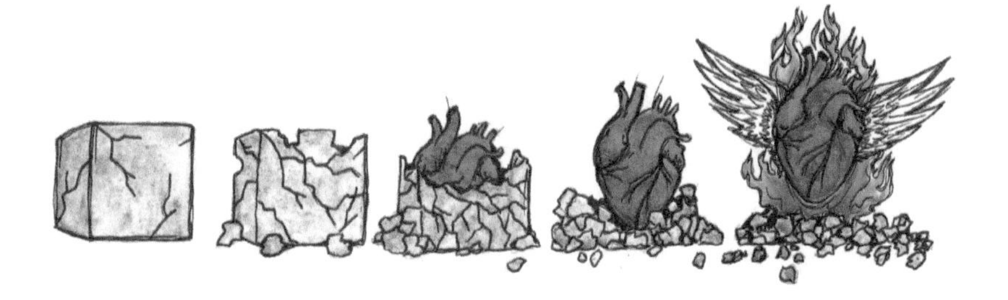

This image came to me when I was moving through some unconscious struggles that had a negative impact on my heart. I have drawn this image repeatedly with the specific intention of healing my "heart space." When I began to intentionally focus on how the heart and mind work together, I began to see just how important it is to heal the heart as well as the mind.

For whatever reason, we might incase our hearts in concrete, perhaps out of protection, fear, or regret. Over time the concrete becomes denser when an issue is not resolved. For a long time, I was unaware that I had let my heart become so incased. However, through the power of art therapy I was prompted to create this image and it allowed me to start imagining the concrete beginning to crack…and eventually a radiant and free heart emerged.

Although this illustration was created in my own imagination, it seems to speak to a universal truth for many. You might share your creative expressions with people, or you might want to keep these thoughts private…either way that is ok. The most important thing is that YOU get your feelings out in some way. Never underestimate the power of your own imagination and creative expression to aid in the healing process!

THE BAG THAT EVERYONE HAS

Along with the visual of the heart incased in concrete, is the concept of your own "bag" that gets bigger with unresolved issues. However, the core idea of this illustration is more about how you can release this heavy bag.

I try my best to not let my bag get so big that it begins to crush me, but there have been times when I was surprised to find things in my bag that I was completely unaware of. And when I learned of things, and tried to release them with anger, retribution, and resentment I found that my bag just got bigger and heavier.

I really thought that if I blamed others for my troubles, it would lessen my pain. But nothing could be further from the truth. So, to shift this victimhood mentality, I used art to express what is possible when you begin looking at those issues with a softer less judgmental perspective. When approaching it in this way, I saw that I had the ability to transform the things in my bag in a much gentler fashion, giving me a sense of appreciation of the lessons that the contents of my bag revealed. I felt better moving through these past wounds with neutrality and acceptance instead of anger and resentment. It is an amazing feeling of freedom when you let your bag go in the spirit of positivity and self-empowerment!

Even with this knowledge, continued maintenance is needed.

THE POWER OF CHOICE

There is another simple yet tough lesson to learn, and that is understanding that we have the power of "Choice." The truth is that we DO have a choice on how we manage our issues, and how we speak to ourselves and others about those problems.

I understand from personal experience that this can be extremely hard to hear. A few years ago, I went through a rough patch where all I could do was think and speak negatively about my problems. I was determined to focus on EVERYTHING that was going wrong. And when someone I trusted told me that I had a choice about how much I thought about my troubles, I got very defensive. I felt offended that someone thought that I LIKED being so negative.

Strangely enough, I had begun to find comfort in those negative thoughts and feelings as they had become FAMILIAR and routine. I was also convinced that by keeping my problems in the front of my mind, I was somehow dealing with them. But in reality, it made it harder to see anything positive while stuck in my own negative tunnel vision.

At one point in time, I was dealing with extremely intrusive thoughts linked to obsessive compulsive disorder (OCD), which made it harder to control my thoughts. It's humbling to accept that sometimes you might need medication to help deal with things that feel out of your control. Many of us might need external aid to get us to the place where even comprehending "choice" is possible.

The idea we have the power of "choice" in how we manage and appreciate our own light and dark aspects of ourselves is ancient, as depicted in the original Cherokee Legend of the dark and light wolf. Ask yourself these questions as you read the original text of this native legend: Which wolf do you feed the most? Do you see value in both wolves? What lessons are they teaching you?

> A group of Cherokee children gathered around their grandfather, filled with excitement and curiosity. That day there had been a tumultuous conflict between two adults and their grandfather was called upon to mediate. The children were eager to hear what their grandfather had to say about it.
>
> One of the children asked a question that puzzled him, "Grandfather, why do people fight?"
>
> Well," the grandfather replied, "we all have two wolves inside us, you see. They live in our chest.
>
> These two wolves are constantly fighting each other." By this time, the children's eyes had grown as big and bright as the moon.
>
> "In our chests too, Grandfather?" asked the second child.
>
> "And in your chest too?" asked a third.
>
> The child who asked the initial question couldn't handle the tension any longer. "Grandfather, which wolf wins?"
>
> The old Cherokee Grandfather explained, - One wolf is dark and evil- he is anger, envy, sorrow, regret, greed, arrogance, self-pity,

guilt, resentment, inferiority, lies, false pride, superiority, and ego." He continued, "The other wolf is light and good- he is joy, peace, love, hope, serenity, humility, kindness, benevolence, empathy, generosity, truth, compassion, and faith. The same fight is going on inside you- and inside every other person, too."

"If you feed them right, they both win. You see, if I only choose to feed the light wolf, the dark wolf will be hiding around every corner waiting for me to become distracted or weak and jump to get the attention he craves. He will always be angry and always fighting the light wolf. But if I acknowledge him, he is happy and the light wolf is happy and we all win. For the dark wolf has many qualities-tenacity, courage, fearlessness, strong willed and great strategic thinking-that I have need of at times and that the light wolf lacks. But the light wolf has compassion, caring, strength and the ability to recognize what is in the best interest of all.

"You see, the light wolf needs the dark wolf at his side. To feed only one would starve the other and they will become uncontrollable. To feed and care for both means they will serve you well and do nothing that is not a part of something greater, something good, something of life. Feed them both and there will be no more internal struggle for your attention. And when there is no battle inside, you can listen to the voices of deeper knowing will guide you in choosing what is right in every circumstance. Peace, my son, is the Cherokee mission in life. A man or woman who has peace inside has everything. A man or woman pulled apart by the war inside him or her has nothing. "How you choose to interact with the opposing forces within you will determine your life. Starve one or the other or guide them both."

A VISUAL FOR FORGIVENESS/LETTING GO

Sometimes the concept of forgiveness is difficult to embrace as it feels like you're giving someone a "pass" that they do not deserve. Rather than saying 'forgive' I began to say to myself that I was willing to "let go."

No one needs to even know that you are doing the work of letting something go. You are doing this for your OWN well-being!

This visual was created at a time when I needed to let go of someone for the benefit of my mental health. What I drew surprised me...

I noticed that the energy of this image was very gentle and not angry. The story of this illustration: **the person who I needed to forgive walked with me to the end dock, then they got into the boat and a calm current set them adrift farther and farther from me. There were no waves or storms, just a gentle drifting until I could no longer see them.**

When thoughts of bitterness resurface (as they often do), I recall this illustration. It seems to bring me peace and a sense of freedom from the righteous anger that once consumed me.

THE CRACK THAT YOU NEVER KNEW WAS THERE.

The cause of this "crack" will be different for everyone. We can all identify with the feeling of trying to fill a pitcher with water, only to find that no matter how much you pour in, it never stays filled.

Considering myself to be somewhat self-aware, I still had no idea that a crack had formed deep within me after a traumatic experience. Although learning about this trauma was very painful, it revealed a huge crack in my soul's pitcher. An undetected crack of that size and depth really ingrained self-sabotaging and self-worth beliefs deep in my subconscious. Even though I was not conscious of this "crack," I could **sense** the despair of feeling like I was never "enough," making it hard to sustain my efforts to live the life I wanted.

Once aware of this crack, I was able to begin the grieving and healing process, eventually reclaiming my power, dignity and self-trust. I can say with much certainty that the crack is now sealed and from now on everything I pour into my pitcher is sustained and builds momentum!

THINGS I HAVE LEARNED OVER THE YEARS...

Disclaimer: Again, I do NOT know all the answers and some of these suggestions will not be for everyone. We all have our own unique path to travel...everyone will have different methods of coping with their beast. I am simply sharing what has worked well for me in my recovery and with the ongoing maintenance of my mental health.

ASKING FOR HELP AND HAVING THE COURAGE TO ACCEPT IT

There is great strength in vulnerability. It takes immense courage to ask for help, especially when it comes to having suicidal thoughts. Several times in my adult life the heaviness of suicidal thoughts moved in like a powerful dark storm. In those moments I felt very helpless and mustering the strength to seek help seemed impossible. Many of us have dark thoughts at times, but if those thoughts keep up for over two weeks more, it is important to ask for help.

When I began to have suicidal thoughts, I focused on the idea of the immense pain that I would cause if I decided to commit suicide, leaving behind a legacy of pain. I truly did not want to hurt the people I love. But like other times there were moments when that factor alone was not enough to keep me safe. When that reason to "hold on" started to fade, I realized that there were two choices, either ask for help or give up. "Do I want to live?" is a very raw and terrifying question to ponder. No wonder people don't ask for help.

The beast can be so tricky when he whispers into your ear convincing you that suicide will finally end your pain. The beast can make suicide feel like a seemingly reasonable option that is **NOT** permanent. However, those moments of desperation, where suicide seemed like a "solution," have always been very brief. Even though I had a "plan" of how I would do it running through my mind, the times when I wanted to carry out those plans were brief and **always** in a moment of crushing hopelessness.

When asking for help... or just talking about the suicidal thoughts that I was beginning to have, I was pulled out of that heavy and dark energy just long enough to move away from the idea that suicide is a viable solution. **Suicide is a permanent solution to a temporary problem.**

Looking back at those frightening moments in my life, I am beyond grateful that I managed to hold on. After each storm, I gained more personal strength, a stronger voice and a deeper appreciation for being alive. Storms DO pass. They always pass!

UNPLUG (TURN OFF THE NOISE)

This one is so important, I thought it needed its own illustration!

When I first encountered the beast the world was not as noisy. Fortunately for me, in my teen years, the analogue world had just begun to cross over to digital. Back then there were no smart phones and the internet was just getting its footing as a mainstay in our homes and schools. As a person who came of age during this technology revolution, I often think about how much harder my struggle would have been if I had to deal with the constant and overwhelming flow of information (negative and positive), cyber bullying, lack of true human connection, and ads and influencers that target your deepest insecurities and fears. When you cannot focus you cannot heal. The more noise you have in your life the harder it is to identify what is causing your problems. To get in touch with your inner self and intuition, it is crucial to unplug.

Sometimes we might think that we are going to find help and a little empathy if we tell the world our problems on social media...and sometimes it is appropriate, but most of the time it only makes you feel worse. The flood of opinions of others only serves to amplify your problems as it just echoes them without constructive feedback. Some people just take the opportunity to tell you **their** problems without acknowledging what you are struggling with, leaving you feeling less seen and heard than before. Sometimes when you seek comfort on such platforms it makes you spiral down with much intensity and speed. When I sense that my "beast" is present, I stay away from social media all together because I know that I am more vulnerable to negativity, and it is a time that I need to seek face to face interactions. **But I understand that this is easier said than done.**

I appreciate how technology has improved my life and I use it to stay connected with loved ones and to run my business, but as a sensitive person, I have a critical need to unplug on a regular basis. I am certainly not immune to phone/social media addiction, and we are all working on decerning the good and bad elements of this technology. I feel that being more conscious of my online interactions has saved me a lot of wasted energy due to self-inflicted anxiety. We are all trying to recognize when we should unplug. Perhaps we should ask ourselves this question before posting or scrolling... "Will this **really** make me feel better?"

MINDFULLNESS

When I have been plugged in too long I focus more on the past and/or the future instead of the present moment. My energy gets more frantic when I neglect intentionally creating quiet moments. The impact is profound when you simply slow down. I use meditation to achieve those moments of quiet stillness. Meditation can take many forms such as listening to specific guided visualizations, practicing structured meditation routines, going for a walk out in nature, or just taking advantage of those rare times that you can just breathe without rushing off to your next obligation!

Some of my best ideas have appeared during these times of mindfulness. I feel so recharged after being in the present moment because that is when I feel the most connected with my authentic self.

FIND AND FOCUS ON YOUR PASSIONS

Do you feel like you have a "calling"? What do you love to do? What makes you feel like you are WHO you are truly meant to be? Do you see yourself having a "life's purpose?" What makes you feel alive? What special things do you bring to the table?

I genuinely believe that my passion to be an artist has saved my life (several times). Creating artwork was one thing that I never stopped doing, even during my deepest struggles. Your passion and purpose can be like a compass that will always point true north if you allow it to guide you.

For some it might take a while to discover what your life's purpose is, but if you are open to it, it will eventually present itself to you. Writing and illustrating this book is very much connected to my mission of creating art to inspire, heal, as well as expressing empathy with the aim to help make this world a better place.

TIME IN NATURE/CONNECTING WITH ANIMALS

Mother Nature, a faithful friend of mine since I was a kid!

I always feel the best when I unplug (literally and metaphorically) and connect with nature. There is a comforting feeling when you feel connected with all the living things around you. You feel like you are a part of something greater than yourself.

I never feel alone when out in the woods or in and around water, in fact I feel like that is when I can really breathe and just "BE" without judgment or expectation. Even being in my backyard with my bare feet touching the grass serves to ground myself in this often-chaotic world. I simply feel my best when I am immersed in a natural setting because the energy is so nurturing and pure.

Also, connecting with the healing power of animals has been a major source of strength and serenity. Something as simple as caring for a pet and/or observing wildlife in their natural habitat can bring a deep sense of peace to a troubled mind.

SPIRITUALITY/RELIGION, WHATEVER FITS FOR YOU!

This is very personal and unique to everyone and not everyone will connect with this concept as a treatment resource and that is OK! Whether it is a specific organized religion or your own concept of spirituality, the idea of believing in something that is beyond you can give you a sense of wonder and the feeling that there is more to life than what you can experience with your five senses. You cannot go wrong when something deeply resonates with you on a soul level, especially if it brings you a sense of belonging and purpose. No matter what spiritual/religious path you choose, the most important thing is that you feel safe and honored.

PRACTICING SELF-CARE/SELF LOVE

It has taken me years to truly understand just how important this is!

Some people might roll their eyes when they hear this because it sounds too simple and a bit trite. Or some think that if you love yourself, you are being arrogant or selfish. But self-love is the cornerstone of healing and cultivating a sense of well-being. It is the foundation of self-esteem and self-worth.

Learning to love who I am (flaws included), has been one of the most difficult lessons to learn. It has been life changing to cultivate more genuine self-love. Being less critical of myself has also boosted my self-confidence. Consider this...it is a very radical act to love yourself unconditionally, especially while living in a culture that thrives on insecurity and the general feeling that you are not enough.

As an adult I made a conscious decision that I was going to change how I spoke to myself and what kind of thoughts I would allow to occupy my mind. After making this decision I saw just how much I criticized myself. I told myself things that I would NEVER say to anyone else because it would be so hurtful. It was not easy to change those ingrained beliefs, and it still takes a lot of maintenance to not fall back into those patterns. Like anything, the way you think and feel about yourself becomes a habit, and with work and consistency you can change any habit! It does get easier over time!

THE POWER OF GRATITUDE/ CREATING A GRATITUDE RITUAL

Like the concept of self-love, practicing gratitude is remarkably simple, yet so incredibly impactful. I feel that practicing acts of appreciation and gratitude resets your outlook on things in general. And now science is backing this up with studies that show that when you practice moments of thankfulness it begins to rewire your brain making it a habit to focus on what is good in your life...especially in tough times.

You can feel gratitude for the simplest things like a delicious meal you ate, a good conversation you had with a friend, or that you have a safe place to live. Personally, I have found that setting aside intentional time to acknowledge the things (big and small) that I am thankful for has changed how I look at the world, and most importantly, how I deal with hardships. In turn, focusing on the good in a situation can open up new ways to perceive a problem and just might reveal a solution that you couldn't see before. In fact, I am so grateful for my beast because it has taught me how to deeply appreciate being alive and healthy.

TRY THIS and see how you feel....it is FREE and EASY!

I do this one simple thing which has greatly impacted my life. Don't knock until you try it!

> I keep a little notebook on my nightstand and every night I write down **at least** three things that I am grateful for from that day. Some days I don't even feel like writing anything down and finding three things to be thankful for is difficult. But sometimes it is the

opposite, and I can't stop writing because there's so much to be thankful for.

I am very disciplined in keeping this "gratitude journal" and it has become part of a nightly ritual. In fact, I feel a bit off if I don't write in it! Since practicing this simple ritual, I have noticed a change in my overall outlook, opening up new ways of approaching challenges.

THE POWER OF ART

You do not have to be "good" at art to create it, just enjoy the feeling you get from the process!

Art in any form can be an incredible source of inspiration and healing. Perhaps we are not as guarded when something is introduced to us through a form of artistic expression. It can open doors in people's minds and hearts because it has a way of connecting to the soul and inspires you to see things differently.

Whether it is film, music, visual art, or the written word, the power of expression can activate your own source of creativity. When you tap into your own creativity you might just find a new way to process and express your own emotions and experiences.

MEDICATIONS/CLINICAL THERAPIES TRADITIONAL AND HOLISTIC

Explore the possibilities!

There is true power in acknowledging that you might need extra help that is beyond your own personal efforts. My relationship with medication/clinical therapies has certainly ebbed and flowed throughout my adult life. I have gone many years without needing medication and other clinical therapies. Then there were times that I knew it was the right decision to use these treatments again.

When it comes to medication it is important to have a health care practitioner that understands you as a whole person. When faced with the possibility of needing medication to treat my depression when I was teenager, I was fortunate to have a psychiatrist who saw me as a whole person, and as an active participant in my treatment. And it helped in finding the right medication for me.

Although I had some adverse reactions to a couple of kinds of medications, and there were a lot of adjustments, we did eventually find a medication that worked well. You know your body best, so it is important to advocate for yourself, or have someone who can be an advocate for you.

THE "HAPPY PILL" MYTH (MY BIGGEST PET PEEVE)

At my annual checkup a nurse asked if I was still taking my "happy pills." I immediately expressed my unease about that label, explaining that the medicine that I am taking does not make me magically happy. Its purpose is to get me to a point where I feel able to begin the work necessary for my healing. Calling it the "happy pill" implies that all you have do is take a pill, without entertaining the idea of making helpful lifestyle changes and/or doing critical inner work. Nothing serves as a "cure all" when it comes to something as complex as your health. You are not a passive participant in any treatment, and that includes treatment for MENTAL health too.

While facing financial and/or personal obstacles in navigating an ever-fluctuating course of treatment, I have implemented holistic elements in my overall plan. I strongly believe that there can be a balance between clinical and holistic approaches. I have used several holistic treatments for my depression since the beginning of my journey, and still use many of those methods today. It comes down to listening to your own intuition, getting the facts from credible and trusted sources, and practicing great self-awareness as you chart out your own treatment plan.

If you struggled like me to gain access to healthcare, please refer to the ACA website included in the resource section in back of this book.

ACTS OF KINDNESS/HELPING OTHERS (CARING FOR LIVING THINGS)

I have found that when I help others I feel better. There have been times when I got so tired of thinking about myself, because when in survival mode you can become extremely self-focused. Although it is necessary to focus on yourself for personal preservation, it is also critical to step out of your own world for a while. Helping others by performing acts of kindness, without expectation of it being reciprocated, can help you achieve this "break" from yourself and can deliver a sense of oneness with all living things.

Science now recognizes that acts of kindness and empathy have proven to lessen loneliness, increase happiness and decrease risk of depression. Your brain releases endorphins when you help someone or something, which reduces pain, boosts your immune system, and increases feelings of euphoria. This is such a great tool to use when dealing with your own mental illness. You can express kindness to humans, animals and even plants in so many different and creative ways. **You will start to see that your light is very contagious!**

PHYSICAL HEALTH/NUTRITION

When I was younger I believed that the mind and body connection was important. But now I am completely convinced that it is one of the most important connections you can have. I really embraced this desire to care for my physical body through conscious self-care efforts.

Through exercise I feel more present in my physical body, and in turn, more stable mentally. Physical movement can do wonders to reduce stress and anxiety as well as to release stagnant emotions(E-motion). Any kind of movement increases self-esteem and the feeling of personal strength. When I have a problem that I am trying to solve, just the simple movement of walking helps me work through issues. And just as important as movement, is getting enough rest and quality sleep!

Also, an important aspect to your health is the fuel you give your body. I have cut out unhealthy foods and unhealthy habits like smoking. With each better choice with what I put in my body, I noticed that my mental health improved simultaneously. But, like anyone else, I will indulge myself from time to time but I am careful to do it in moderation.

Science supports the paramount importance of mind, body, and spirit congruence. I do my best to avoid things that damage my mind, body, or spirit. No one is perfect, nor should you expect perfection...sometimes it comes down to being honest with yourself and accepting that some things are just not worth the damage they cause.

PEOPLE WHO SUPPORT YOU

Who do you trust? Who consistently supports you? Who always has your highest good in mind? Who is honest enough to give you tough love when needed?

These are the people who you deserve to surround yourself with and these are the people who can serve as motivators and cheerleaders in your healing process! These people come in many forms such as family, friends, neighbors, teachers, coaches, clergy and mentors. The bottom line is that you trust them and that they have your best interest at heart... and someday YOU can be the person who provides that unconditional love and care for someone else who needs help.

THEN AND NOW

A LETTER FROM CAIT'S MOM THEN

Dear Reader,

This could never happen to us...but it did. As close as we have always been, I was shocked to learn that Cait had put an artist's knife to her wrist the night before our first psychiatric appointment. If you, yourself, or someone else you know, is in the position of being the person to help a loved one suffering from depression, gather your courage and energy and begin to "challenge the beast."

You don't have to be an expert in psychology to begin to shrink the beast. You already have it in you, right now, to meet the challenge. To help someone who's depressed, here are some things I learned from the experience...

Begin by recognizing that there is a problem. Take the initiative and follow Cait's advice in the book.

Whatever you are now, start thinking of yourself as an OBSERVER so you can be a good REPORTER to the Dr., counselor, or teacher about what is happening. Keep a journal.

Be a positive COMMUNICATOR and LISTENER. Make it clear you are committed to helping them to wellness. (Cait always asked me "Are you going to give up on me? I always answered, "never.")

Be prepared to be a COORDINATOR of whatever is necessary such as appointments, medication refills. You may feel overwhelmed as they rely on you in so many ways, but you are not alone. Enlist help from others such as family, friends, teachers, or anyone else willing to assist. You will be surprised at the help and concern others will offer.

You'll soon learn how widespread this illness called depression is in our society today. Approach the school for help so time lost at school can be kept to a minimum. Look into Family Leave from your job if you find it necessary to stay home for a period of time. This was a lifesaver for us.

Trust your own judgement and intuition. You know your loved one better than anybody. Follow the Dr.'s advice, but don't be afraid to disagree or question. Your opinion and ideas are invaluable. (We replaced a sleeping pill that gave Cait nightmares with an herbal remedy...and it worked.)

Don't underestimate the power of nurturing to heal the person and shrink the beast. I believe this is just as important as medicine and counseling. Start thinking of yourself as a NURTURER and experience the good feelings you get in return. Along with doing these loving and caring things, goes the gradual "release" toward independence, which is the goal.

Your battle with the beast of depression won't be an easy one but you'll find the journey itself has many rewards...we did and so can you!

NOW

A Mom's point of view...

Fortunately, for both of us, Cait and I have maintained a very close relationship as she moved through the life of a teenager to her present adult life as an artist. Of course, as in anybody's life, there have been ups and downs on her path to adulthood, but mostly UPs!

Cait has always remained true to her original self and her perceived "purpose in life."

*Still an artist and entrepreneur 24/7

*Always a beautiful, creative, intense, passionate, funny, kind, nature loving person

*A devoted daughter, Auntie, and steadfast friend to many

*Very concerned about the state of the world

*Intensely willing to "do the work" to understand herself and be the best she can be for herself and others

In a nutshell, Cait has basically never given up on herself, her work, her life's purpose and has grown as an artist in self-confidence, along with a true zest for life!

"Cait, I agree with you, that now is the time, more than ever, to revive your original book <u>Conquering the Beast Within</u>. Put it back out into the world again!! Reach out to help others, while not pretending to have all the answers, but just to share and be an inspiration to others for hope and recovery."

For Cait to revisit those tough teen years and dive in again to make herself "available" to others in their time of need is truly brave! As her mother, I am so proud of her now for having the courage to be vulnerable...then and now.

A LETTER FROM CAIT'S BROTHER- THEN

Dear Reader,

At the time Cait began going through her depression, I was 16. I didn't really know what was going on. My life was busy with school, work, and sports. It was football season. When I did begin to understand the situation, dealing with it was just too hard to handle.

I was afraid of disrupting my own life. Family counseling was pointless because I wasn't the crazy one and going to see Cait in the hospital was scary. I wondered what my friends were thinking and saying. Sometimes it seemed she had brought it all on herself.

Looking back with some maturity, Cait's situation seems different to me now. If I could go back in time, I would "be there" for her and I would also listen and believe her without judgement. One thing I know for sure is a depressed person needs the whole family to recover.

NOW

During the first publication of Cait's book I was a teenager. Like most teenagers I was searching for myself. If you would have told me that I would be a public-school superintendent, I would have said you were crazy. You never know where life takes you and I have dedicated my career to serving all students in our public schools.

Being an educator requires me to draw upon my own experiences to provide the best guidance for all students in my school. Everyone has highs and lows in their lives, and it is up to us to help and support students in good times and bad.

Whether it is sports figures, musicians, influencers, older siblings, parents, etc..... Young students often look to others for inspiration and direction in their lives as they are attempting to form their identity. "Conquering the Beast Within" offers inspiration for those students struggling with their feelings. For many students

Cait's personal story is their first glimpse into understanding that they are not alone.

No student should ever have to struggle alone, and my hope is that a student who reads Cait's book is inspired to ask someone they trust for help. At each school district that I have had the privilege of serving, I have donated a copy of "Conquering the Beast Within" to the school library collection. If just one student checks Cait's book out and it makes a difference for them it is a great day.

A LETTER FROM CAIT'S DAD THEN

Dear Reader,

The easiest thing for a man to do when his child or loved one suffers from depression is to avoid the entire situation. We pretend it doesn't exist and don't want to talk or admit anything is wrong. We feel by avoiding this uncomfortable emotional experience, it will go away. The lyrics to Paul Simon's song pointed out that there are fifty ways to leave your lover. Well, I believe there are just as many ways that men can leave their families and friends suffering from depression.

Why do we act this way? I've suffered myself and done research on the subject and found that men, in general, see depression as a weakness. We view it as unmanly and shameful. We're angry with a depressed person because we believe or feel they should be able to "pull themselves out of it." We tend to hide our own depression and seldom seek help and wonder why others should. We usually just live with it and silently suffer, and in some cases, end it all.

The most important thing a person can do is to put the welfare of those struggling with depression ahead of their own fears, anxieties, and preconceived notions about the illness. But I want you to know, it takes real courage to open up and become a team player in the recovery process.

I personally didn't have the courage to help Cait through her darkest times. Fortunately, she had others to accept the responsibility and I'll be forever grateful. I couldn't talk about depression then with Cait or anyone else and couldn't be there emotionally for her either. But I did try to help her in my own way.

If your loved one is facing depression, seek ways to help them. If you can't talk about it, don't disappear. If you can't be there emotionally, be there physically and pay attention. Stay in their lives and resist the temptation to avoid their struggle. Don't take your own anger and feeling out on them. Build something together, go places, grow things, surf the net, make plans, make commitments. But most of all be patient.

NOW

After the first book, Cait has remained consistent in her mission to help those dealing with depression. As a follow-up to her publication, she has presented several lectures and interviews nationwide. Not an easy task considering she must relive some of the uncomfortable events and explore these feelings to help others.

I have witnessed her persistence in following her creative path despite many obstacles in life. Cait has also been unselfish with her time by getting involved in community and political activities. She has been courageous in her pursuits.

She has also inspired me by bringing my own depression into focus. While at a presentation with hundreds of participants she was taking questions. For example, one person asked if she thought depression was hereditary. She turned and pointed to me sitting in the audience and said, "thanks Dad!" The audience laughed at her lighthearted explanation, but it was true. Although it was a serious question, she answered with her usual honesty about depression.

I have witnessed the impact of the original <u>Conquering the Beast Within</u> book and look forward to an even more powerful revision.

WHERE THERE IS HELP THERE IS HOPE...

Call/Text Hotline Resources.

Confidentially connect with Trained Professionals 24/7

***National Suicide and Crisis Hotline CALL or Text 988**
*(Languages: English, Spanish)**

Additional specific Hotlines:

Substance Abuse and/or Mental Health- Call 1-800-662-4357

National LGBTQ hotline(general)- Call lifeline 1-800-273-8255 or text HOME at 741741

LGBTQ Youth Hotline- Call 1-800-246-7743

Trevorlifeline- Call 1-866-488-7386 or text START to 678678

Trans Lifeline- Call 1-877-565-8860 (US) 877-330-6366 (Canada)

Textline for People of Color, Youth and Adult – text STEVE to 741741

Additional ONLINE Resources for help, information, and hope:

National Institute of Mental Health(NIMH): ***nimh.nih.gov***

National Alliance on Mental Illness(NAMI): ***nami.org***

Mental Health Resources for Immigrants:
informedimmigrant.com

Mental Health Resources for Veterans: ***mentalhealth.va.gov***

Holistic Mental Health Resources: ***mindful.org***

Substance Abuse and Mental Health Services Administration:
samhsa.gov

Emotional Support Animal Education and Registration:
esaregistartion.org

Resources for Accessing Health Insurance/Medication Prescriptions: ***Healthcare.gov***

Health Insurance Resources- Affordable Care Act (ACA):
affordablehealthplans.org

MORE ABOUT THE AUTHOR AND ILLUSTRATOR CAIT IRWIN:

Cait Irwin is a professional artist as well as a published author, entrepreneur, naturalist, and world traveler. Being an artist and having a deep connection with the natural world have always been two major constants in her life. Her artwork is prolific, spanning a wide spectrum of mediums, styles, and subject matter. From murals to sculpture, she does it all!

At age fourteen Cait wrote and illustrated "Conquering the Beast Within," a memoir about her personal experience with severe depression (Published by Times Books 1999). During that time, she also started her first art business called "Reality Impaired." In her own way, she was rebelling against a culture that says that being an artist is an unrealistic career path.

In 2004 she co-authored a follow up book called "Monochrome Days." (Published by Oxford University Press) Cait toured extensively to promote her books and was the keynote speaker for numerous events focusing on mental health, the healing power of art and self-expression and recovery.

She graduated from Northland College in 2003 with a bachelor's in Studio Art, minoring in Environmental Studies/Native American Studies.

Currently, Cait is the owner of Irwin Artworks LLC and is in her 10th year of operation and is based in Southwest Iowa. Her company showcases her work, ranging from large murals and illustration projects to sculptures made from recycled materials. She has also established a strong online presence where she sells a large amount of her work. Cait also travels to a variety of established Artist residencies as well as designing her own. She is constantly gathering inspiration from the world around her and is always on the lookout for new projects with new challenges. **See more of her work at Irwinartworks.com.**

Cait also sells a high volume of original art as well as prints through her Etsy shop at irwinartworks.etsy.com.

BOOK A PRESENATION WITH CAIT

Cait is available for presentations where she speaks from the heart and offers a powerful visual element through her own artwork. She is a talented and charismatic public speaker and has been a keynote speaker for various national and local organizations, as well as for schools and online forums. Her authentic and approachable energy is unique and inspires any group she engages with as she has the inane ability to connect with all walks of life, lending a compassionate ear while telling her own story with courage, vulnerability and humor. Cait is NOT a mental health professional. She simply offers a personal perspective of being a patient and survivor of suicide.

Cait can also offer a book selling and signing portion of her presentation if requested.

For more information and to book Cait email: Info@irwinartworks.com

Visit Irwinartworks.com to learn more about Cait.

Previous Praise for book: Self-published "Depression, Challenge the Beast within Yourself and Win."

"I was utterly charmed by this wonderful little book-and deeply moved. Her words and drawings leap off the page and make you care. And, as is if that weren't enough, the information is comprehensive and balanced."

-Fredrick K Goodwin, M.D. Professor of Psychiatry at the George Washington University, and former director of the National institute of Mental Health

"In Offering readers a vivid image Cait Irwin allows those with depression to not feel defined by their disorder. A book for those of all ages, it paints the isolation, fear and misunderstanding of mental illness in provoking and recognizable strokes. A work of compassion and hope."

-Laurie Flynn, Executive Director, NAMI

"Cait Irwin's direct and honest portrayal of her teenage challenge with depression is a most significant contribution to the field of mental health. It is a book certain to speak to young people and their families who are confronting the devastating effects of this illness."

-Ione Jenson, author of Emerging Women, and Women Alone.

"Cait Irwin's book should find a ready acceptance in the corporate world especially among managers and personnel officers. Many employers are reluctant to seek help from professionals for fear of being seen as "unable to cope with their problems." Her book deals straightforwardly with depression in a compassionate manner and speaks to why mental and emotional illnesses should be accepted and treated like any other illness."

-Bill Meyer, Ph.D. retired CEO Int'l Psychological Consulting Firm

"It's an inspiring and thought-provoking book. Cait's spirit and wisdom will help thousands of others. I don't recall ever reading a better publication on depression."

-Stan Maliszeski Ph.D., Head of Guidance and Counseling- Omaha Public Schools

"This book is the most wonderful therapeutic tool for understanding and giving insight into depression that I have seen in my ten years of working with children and adolescents."

-Jeff Loeb MA, L.P.C.,L.M.F.T Children's Medical Center, Tulsa, OK